Simulation and Test-System of Vehicle Body CAN Bus - A Project Report

Gerardine Mary (Ed.)

Simulation and Test-System of Vehicle Body CAN Bus - A Project Report

LAP LAMBERT Academic Publishing

Impressum / Imprint

Bibliografische Information der Deutschen Nationalbibliothek: Die Deutsche Nationalbibliothek verzeichnet diese Publikation in der Deutschen Nationalbibliografie; detaillierte bibliografische Daten sind im Internet über http://dnb.d-nb.de abrufbar.

Alle in diesem Buch genannten Marken und Produktnamen unterliegen warenzeichen-, marken- oder patentrechtlichem Schutz bzw. sind Warenzeichen oder eingetragene Warenzeichen der jeweiligen Inhaber. Die Wiedergabe von Marken, Produktnamen, Gebrauchsnamen, Handelsnamen, Warenbezeichnungen u.s.w. in diesem Werk berechtigt auch ohne besondere Kennzeichnung nicht zu der Annahme, dass solche Namen im Sinne der Warenzeichen- und Markenschutzgesetzgebung als frei zu betrachten wären und daher von jedermann benutzt werden dürften.

Bibliographic information published by the Deutsche Nationalbibliothek: The Deutsche Nationalbibliothek lists this publication in the Deutsche Nationalbibliografie; detailed bibliographic data are available in the Internet at http://dnb.d-nb.de.

Any brand names and product names mentioned in this book are subject to trademark, brand or patent protection and are trademarks or registered trademarks of their respective holders. The use of brand names, product names, common names, trade names, product descriptions etc. even without a particular marking in this works is in no way to be construed to mean that such names may be regarded as unrestricted in respect of trademark and brand protection legislation and could thus be used by anyone.

Coverbild / Cover image: www.ingimage.com

Verlag / Publisher:
LAP LAMBERT Academic Publishing
ist ein Imprint der / is a trademark of
OmniScriptum GmbH & Co. KG
Heinrich-Böcking-Str. 6-8, 66121 Saarbrücken, Deutschland / Germany
Email: info@lap-publishing.com

Herstellung: siehe letzte Seite /
Printed at: see last page
ISBN: 978-3-659-63009-5

DEDICATED TO

OUR PARENTS

AND

Prof. GERARDINE IMMACULATE MARY

ACKNOWLEDGEMENT

It is with great satisfaction and honor that I present my thesis on the project under taken during 7th and 8th semesters, for the award of Undergraduate Bachelor of Technology degree at VIT University Vellore.

We are very thankful to Professor **Gerardine Immaculate Mary** for being our mentor, guide, inspiration and constant motivation
 for our project. She has been the corner stone of our project and has guided us during times of doubts and uncertainties. Her ideas, inspirations, knowledge and her expertise have helped us in making a nascent idea of ours' into a full-fledged project.

We are also thankful to **Mr. Karthik Shanmugam** (Engineer at Robert Bosch, a contact provided by our mentor) for helping us out on a completely unknown platform and providing much useful literature resources. We are also thankful to all the professors of our department especially for being a constant source of inspiration and motivation during course of the project. We also express our heartiest thanks to **Mr. S. Sivanantham** and **Mr. G. Boopalan** our project co-coordinators for their timely guidance and field expertise. We offer our heartiest thanks to all our friends and family for their help and co-operation. Another person that deserves greatly to be acknowledged is our lab technician **Mr. V. Karthikeyan** for offering his expertise with hardware diagnostics and his good advice.

Last but not the least, our sincere thanks to Professor Mr. Modi Pandu Ranga Prasad for helping us in getting the best guide we could get for our project. We are grateful to our mentor for helping us in correcting our thesis. We would like to thank all those who go through our thesis and we would be greatly elated if anyone finds it helpful for future reference.

PALETI SRINATH
(09BEC370)

&

KANDURI SRINIVAS
(09BEC220)

ii

ABSTRACT

The CAN bus which has been widely used in electric vehicle control system have many characteristics such as high transmission efficiency, high reliability, good real-time feature and so on. CAN is serial communications protocol which efficiently supports distributed real time control with very high level of security. **CANoe** v7.6 which is the product of a German company Vector is a practical and powerful tool for system design and analysis of CAN networks and others (FlexRay, LIN etc.). Firstly, a design scheme of simulation and test system for vehicle body CAN bus network is brought forward, which mainly includes the topology of network, the hierarchical model of network and the selection of bus baud rate. Secondly, a method of how to use **CANoe** to construct the simulation and test environment for vehicle body CAN bus system is implemented. Finally, the simulation and test system for vehicle body CAN bus is completed by **CANoe** v7.6. The results are also be verified on Flexdevel board. The FlexDevel boards consist of MPC5567 chip and many input ports and output ports. Experiments that are done demonstrate that the development method of simulation and test system is feasible.

TABLE OF CONTENTS

LIST OF FIGURES

LIST OF ABBREVIATIONS

CAN	Control Area Network
ECU	Electronic Control Unit
IEEE	Institute of electronics and electrical engineers
ISO	International Standards Organization
Mbps	Megabits per second
CSMA/CD	Carrier Sense Multiple Access, Collision Detect
WLAN	Wireless Local Area Network
LIN	Local Inter connect Network
SPI	Serial Peripheral Interface
HS Bus	High Speed Bus
PWM	Pulse Width Modulation
LED	Light Emitting Diode
LCD	Liquid Crystal Display
EMS	Engine Monitoring System
Msg	Message
IDE	Integrated Development Environment
USB	Universal Serial Bus
RX	Receive
TX	Transmit

CHAPTER 1

INTRODUCTION

1.1 OVERVIEW

Now-a-day's every system is automated in order to face new challenges, in the present days automated systems have less manual operations, flexibility, reliability and accurate, due to this demand every field prefers automated control systems especially in the field of electronics, automated systems are giving good performance . In order to implement such a system it has to give promising results in the software platform.

Software platforms are usually equipped with all the modules that are present in the hardware. In this project, a vehicle body can bus is designed so that it reflects real time scenario of the various control units in the vehicle. The CAN (controller area network) is a serial communication protocol which efficiently supports distributed real time control with very high level of security.

CAN is of ISO standard 11898 which is defined a physical layer of baud rates up-to 1Mbps. In this we create a real time scenario of various control units of a vehicle and we will study various functionalities of control units.

1.2 MOTIVATION FOR THESIS

With rapid development in automobile technology around the world many ECUs (electronic control units) were developed to improve the quality, comfort, security and safety of automobiles and the people using them. The definition for an ECU is: *"In automotive electronics, **electronic control unit (ECU)** is a generic term for any embedded system that controls one or more of the electrical system or subsystems in a motor vehicle."*

Actual ECU developing seems to be more expensive and may not yield the satisfactory results. Building a software prototype of an actual ECU however is still possible to illustrate the effectiveness of intended application. In this project, CAN technology is used to integrate the ECUs to illustrate effectiveness of ECU functionalities.

1

CAN is of ISO standard 11898. As such CAN has a great potential for incorporation of ECUs for control purposes, monitoring purposes and safety purposes.

The motivation for doing this project was primarily an interest in undertaking a challenging project in an interesting area of research. The opportunity to learn about a new area of designing not covered in lectures was appealing. This is possibly an area we might study at post graduate level.

1.3 ORGANIZATION FOR THESIS

This thesis is divided into 6 chapters.

Chapter 1, gives introduction and motivation for "SIMULATION AND TEST SYSTEM FOR VECHILE BODY CAN BUS."

Chapter 2, deals with literature study that includes CANoe software, CAN protocol, CANcaseXL, FLEXDEVEL etc.

Chapter 3, covers design / programming methodologies suggested in literature and discusses earlier work done in CAN networks.

Chapter 4, describes in detail how software version can be tested on hardware.

Chapter 5, deals with the results of the project.

Chapter 6, concludes the thesis and future works.

CHAPTER   2
LITERATURE SYUDY

2.1 CAN

2.1.1 INRODUCTION

In February of 1986, Robert Bosch GmbH introduced the new serial bus system Controller Area Network (CAN) at the Society of Automotive Engineers (SAE) congress. It was the time for one of the most successful network protocols ever. Today, almost every latest passenger car manufactured throughout the world is built along with at least one CAN network. It also used in other types of vehicles, from trains to ships, as well as in industrial purposes, CAN is one of the most dominating bus protocols and it may be even the leading serial bus system worldwide with more and more features getting added on.

In the early 1980s, engineers at Bosch were examining to evaluate the existing serial bus systems regarding their possible use in passenger cars. Because none of the existing network protocols were able to satisfy the requirements of the automotive engineers, Uwe Kiencke began the development of a new serial bus system in 1983. The new bus protocol was mainly supposed to add new functionality in addition to that the reduction of wiring harnesses was just a by-product, but not the driving force for the development of CAN. Engineers from Mercedes-Benz and Intel got involved in the specification phase of the new serial bus system. Professor Dr. Wolfhard Lawrenz from the University of Applied Science in Braunschweig-Wolfenbüttel, Germany, who was hired as a consultant, gave the name 'Controller Area Network'. Professor Dr. Horst Wettstein of University of Karlsruhe provided academic assistance and gave a helping hand.

In February of 1986, CAN was born: at the SAE congress in Detroit, the new bus system developed by Bosch was introduced as 'Automotive Serial Controller Area Network'. Uwe Kiencke, Siegfried Dais and Martin Litschel introduced the multi-master network protocol. It was based on a non-destructive arbitration mechanism, which would

3

grant bus access to the message with the highest priority without any delays. There was no central bus master. Furthermore, the fathers of CAN – the individuals mentioned above plus Bosch employees Wolfgang Borst, Wolfgang Botzenhard, Otto Karl, Helmut Schelling, and Jan Unruh – had implemented several error detection mechanisms. The error handling also included the automatic disconnection of faulty bus nodes in order to keep up the communication between the remaining nodes. The transmitted messages were not identified by the node address of the transmitter or the receiver of the message (as in almost all other bus systems), but rather by their content. The identifier representing the content of the message also had the function of specifying the priority of the message within the system.

A lot of presentations and publications describing this innovative communication protocol followed, until in mid 1987 – two months ahead of schedule – Intel delivered the first CAN controller chip, the 82526. It was the very first hardware implementation of the CAN protocol. In only four years, an idea had become reality. Shortly thereafter, Philips Semiconductors introduced the 82C200. These two earliest ancestors of the CAN controllers were quite different concerning acceptance filtering and message handling. On one hand, the Full CAN concept favored by Intel required less CPU load from the connected micro-controller than the Basic CAN implementation chosen by Philips. On the other hand, the Full CAN device was limited regarding the number of messages that could be received. The Basic CAN controller also required less silicon. In today's CAN controllers, the 'grandchildren', very often different concepts of acceptance filtering and message handling have been implemented in the same module, making the misleading terms Basic CAN and Full CAN obsolete.

2.1.2 CAN ARCHITECTURE

The growth of control systems in vehicle caused the growth of ECUs (Electronic Control Units) that require intercommunication. This intercommunication is achieved by networking technology known as CAN (Controller Area Network).

4

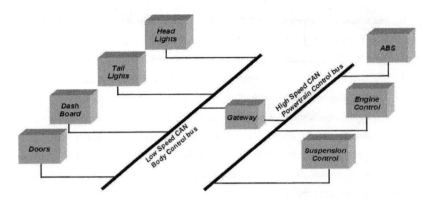

Figure 2.1

CAN is a contention based communication media, where each ECU must see that the bus is not busy before sending its CAN data frame across the bus. This utilizes a procedure known as CSMA/CD (Carrier Sense Multiple Access, Collision Detect). Simply put, The ECU's share one wire, and must contend for the use of that wire to communicate with the other ECU's. As the name implies, the system is multiple access of the ECU's to the wire (or bus), and if an ECU wishes to transfer data onto the bus, it must sense if the bus is not in use by another ECU. If the bus is busy, then that ECU will hold the data until the bus is not busy, and then transmit.

The Collision Detect comes into play when two or more ECU's, at the exact same time, sense then transmit. In this scenario, the data from the different ECU's will collide and cause corruption of that data. CAN utilise a routine that senses this and allow the high priority information (e.g. wheel speed) to have throughput, while lower priority information (e.g. engine temp) will be slightly delayed. This is very similar to computer networking technology used in our offices and homes, e.g. Ethernet.

With this type of architecture, some information contending for the bus can be very low priority, not requiring time critical response. To avoid this data from cluttering up the contention arrangement for a time critical data bus, lower priority information bearing ECU's are isolated to a separate CAN bus and connected to the higher priority

5

bus via a Gateway. The Gateway acts as a filter to control data passed from the Body Control CAN bus to the Powertrain Control CAN bus, and vice versa. In Figure above, this is shown where the Powertrain Control bus is the high priority information carrier, and the Body Control bus is the low priority information carrier.

2.1.3 CAN-ECU INTERFACE

In today's vehicles, most of the ECU's are interconnected via the CAN bus. Figure, illustrates the structure of an ECU, where it contains a Microcontroller and a network interface in the form of the CAN Controller and the CAN Transceiver. The Microcontroller is the central controller that contains the embedded control program, such as Engine control or Suspension control. The CAN Controller acts as the network interface, where it extracts data from the Microcontroller to be transferred to other ECU's, and puts that data into frames to be transferred across the CAN bus. The CAN Transceiver sets up the electrical signalling to transfer data across the CAN bus. Connecting a CAN controller to a microcontroller is analogous to connecting an Ethernet interface to a PC.

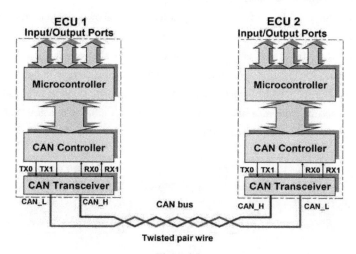

Figure 2.2

6

2.1.4 The CAN Frame and its Data Field

When control data (e.g. engine speed) is needed for transfer to another ECU, the Microcontroller sends this data to the CAN Controller, where it puts it into a frame that identifies where the data is to go, as well as scales the data to information concerning its control function. Figure below shows a very basic structure of a CAN frame. Here, it can be seen that the header contains the Identifier and info on the size of the Data Field. The Identifier tells the rest of the system what the data is, e.g. Engine Parameters. The Data Field contains the actual parameters e.g. engine speed, temperature, navigator, lights, engine status oil pressure. The Trailer contains error checking info and establishes the end of frame.

Header	Data Field	Trailer
Identifier & Size of Data Field	Control Signals, e.g. Engine parameters	Error checking & End of Frame
(approx 20 to 35 bits)	(approx 8 to 64 bits)	(approx 25 bits)

Figure 2.3

2.1.5 CAN Physical bus and Electric signal

Typically the CAN bus is two wires twisted together to allow simple electrical noise immunity. When the CAN frame is to be transferred, the electrical signal transmitted from the CAN Transceiver is a dual differential digital burst of data that makes up the CAN frame. The electrical appearance of the CAN frame is illustrated in figure below, where CAN_H (CAN High) and CAN_L (CAN Low) represent the same information in opposite polarity from each other. That is to say, this is a differential signal. This is a view on a two channel oscilloscope of the signal.

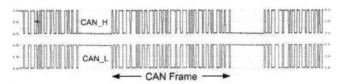

Figure 2.4

Here it can be seen that when the bus is not busy CAN_H and CAN_L are the same voltage level of approx 2.5 V (they are offset a bit for illustration). When there is data, CAN_H increases it level, while CAN_L decreases its level. This is sensed at the receiver part of the CAN Transceiver as a differential signal. This facilitates a simple noise immunity method, where if there is a noise spike on CAN_H, there will be an equal but opposite spike on CAN_L. Therefore, the differential result remains the same.

2.1.6 CAN Protocol

The CAN protocol is an international standard defined in the ISO 11898-1. Besides the CAN protocol itself, the conformance test for the CAN protocol is defined in the ISO 16845-1, which guarantees the interoperability of the CAN protocol controller chips. In 2012, the classic CAN protocol has been improved. The improved CAN data link layer protocol is also known as CAN FD (flexible data-rate).

CAN is based on the "broadcast communication mechanism", which is based on a message-oriented transmission protocol. It defines message contents rather than stations and station addresses. Every message has a message identifier, which is unique within the whole network since it defines content and also the priority of the message. This is important when several stations compete for bus access (bus arbitration). As a result of the content-oriented addressing scheme a high degree of system and configuration flexibility is achieved. It is easy to add stations to an existing CAN network without making any hardware or software modifications to the present stations as long as the new stations are purely receivers. This allows for a modular concept and also permits the reception of multiple data and the synchronization of distributed processes. Also, data transmission is not based on the availability of specific types of stations, which allows simple servicing and upgrading of the network.

2.2 CANoe

2.2.1 Introduction

CANoe is a universal development, test and analysis environment for CAN bus systems, which is made available to all project participants over the entire development process. The system producer is supported in functional distribution, functional checking and integration of the overall system. The supplier obtains an ideal test environment by simulation of the remainder of the bus and environment.

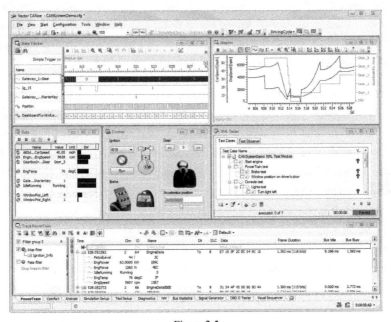

Figure 2.5

2.2.2 CANoe three phase model

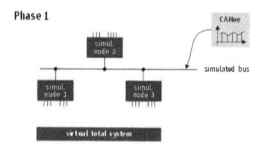

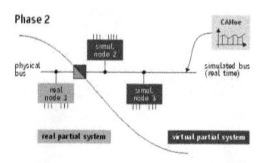

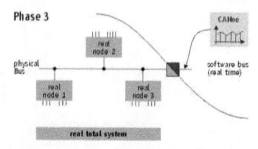

Figure 2.6

a) Virtual total system:

This system is entirely software oriented where each of the ECUs created are virtual in nature . This system is mostly used for designing , studying , analyzing and testing of new ECUs .

b) Real partial system:

This system is partly software oriented and partly hardware oriented , where one or more ECUs can be virtual or real. This system is mostly used for designing , studying , analyzing and testing of new ECUs (virtual) to go hand in hand with the existing ECUs.

c) Real total system:

This system is entirely hardware oriented where each of the ECUs are real in nature . This system is mostly used for studying , analyzing and testing .

2.2.3 Protocols , Bus systems and options supported by CANoe

> **Bus systems:**

CAN, LIN, MOST, FlexRay, Ethernet, WLAN,
Car2x ITS G5, AFDX®, J1708

> **Protocols:**

IP, CANopen, J1939, ISO 11783, NMEA 2000, J1587, MCnet, GMLAN, K-Line, CANaerospace and ARINC810/812/825/826. Others upon request.

> **Options:**

AMD, XCP, SCOPE, DiVa

Only one tool for all development and test tasks

> Easy automated testing

> Simulate and test ECU diagnostics

> Detect and correct error situations early in the development process

> User-friendly graphic and text-based evaluation of results

2.3 CAN CaseXL

2.3.1 Introduction

The CAN Case XL is a USB interface with a powerful 32-bit 64MHzmicrocontroller from ATMEL with ARM7 core and two SJA1000 CAN controllers from Philips. It can process CAN messages with either 11-bit or 29–bit identifiers. It is also capable of generating and detecting error frames on bus. Basically the CAN CaseXL is an interfacing or a bridging medium between the software CANoe and the real time hardware.

Figure 2.7

2.3.2 CAN CaseXL connectors

The CANcaseXL has the following connectors:

☐ USB connector for the usage with PC in Interface Mode

☐ Binder connector (type 712) for power supply, synchronization and trigger

☐ two D-SUB9 connectors for independent CAN/LIN operation

2.4 FLEXDEVEL

2.4.1 Introduction

The *FlexDevel* is a universal and powerful developer platform for easy and fast usage of the MPC5567 for implementing your own test applications, gateways or any other software function, because all interfaces and the most needed features are already supported by the supplied software library. With this platform FlexRay systems for laboratory usage can be built up easily. The huge amount of interfaces enables solutions for a wide range of applications. *FlexDevel* supports one 100Mbit/s Ethernet, one FlexRay communication interface with two channels, two CAN, one LIN, one RS232 and two SPI bus interfaces. Additionally *FlexDevel* provides several input and output signals that can be used to read sensor signals or to control specific hardware

Figure 2.8

2.4.2 Applications

FlexDevel is designed for a use in laboratories in schools, universities or enterprises. The intended use for the *FlexDevel* is e.g. in education or development and for testing new functions in a laboratory environment.

2.4.3 Technical Features

- Freescale PowerPC with integrated FlexRay Controller (MPC5567)
- 2 FlexRay-Channels (channel A and B)
- 2 CAN HS bus interfaces
- Switchable termination resistors (via DIP-switches) for CAN and FlexRay
- Wakeup/Sleep-support (wakeup possible via CAN/FlexRay, push-button or permanent on)
- 1 LIN, 1 RS232,2 SPI ,1 100Mbit/s Ethernet
- 8 digital inputs
- 8 digital outputs (also usable as PWM)
- 8 analog inputs, 8 PWM output
- 2 H-Bridges for control of actuators
- 8 individual usable LEDs
- 2 individual usable push-buttons
- 1 slot for a LCD-module
- Power supply range: 9-16V

2.4.4 Pin Diagram

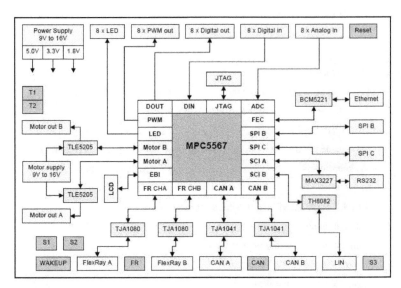

Figure 2.9

2.4.5 POWER SUPPLY

The valid range of the external power supply for the *FlexDevel* is within 9V – 16V DC. The power supply input of the *FlexDevel* is reverse protected. Internal voltage regulators generate the operating voltages out of this supply voltage. The FlexRay, CAN and LIN bus drivers support an UBAT supply input that supplies the bus driver in sleep mode. The respective UBAT supply pin of the bus driver ICs are directly connected to the reverse protected power supply.

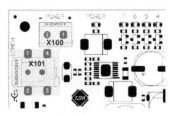

Figure 2.10

15

2.4.6 DIGITAL IN

The digital inputs are protected by a 2.2kohm resistor against over voltage till 16V. The nominal input level is 5V the input impedance 2.2kohm.The input can be given from a DC power supply.

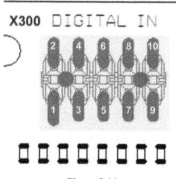

Figure 2.11

2.4.7 CAN

The *FlexDevel* µController MPC5567 supports five CAN interfaces, from CAN A to E. The *FlexDevel* uses the interface CAN A and B.

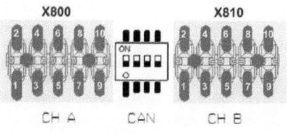

Figure 2.12

CHAPTER 3

BLOCK DIAGRAMS AND SOFTWARE IMPLEMENTATION

3.1 Creating a CANoe Application

In this step-by-step, we will develop different applications that primarily reflect the CANoe development process.

3.1.1 Create a New Directory

1) Before starting up CANoe, create a new directory called "new1" to contain the new configuration. Consider locating this directory close to the CANoe application directory.

2) Start CANoe and use the main menu to go to File → New Configuration. A prompt appears to select a template. Choose the one that fits the situation, or if you are not sure, select the default template.

3) Go to File → Save Configuration As. Name the file "new1.cfg" using a path to the new directory name. Then click [OK].

3.2 CANoe Development – Six Step Process

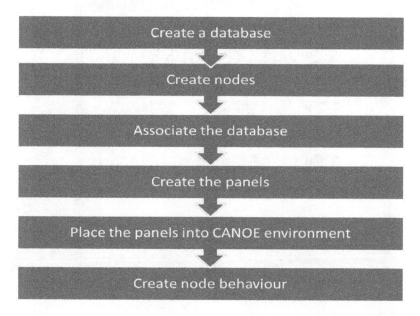

Figure 3.1

3.3 Create a Database

3.3.1 Create the Database File

1) On the CANoe toolbar, click the CANdb++ Editor button (the one with 4 interconnected red nodes) to launch the integrated database tool.

2) In CANdb++ Editor, go to File → Create Database. A prompt appears to select a template. Choose the one that fits the situation, or if you are not sure, select the empty template. For this tutorial, we will select the empty template.

3) Save the file as a DBC file called "new1.dbc" in the directory just created.

18

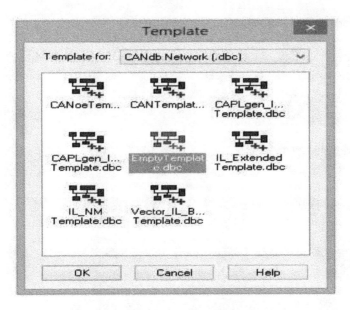

Figure 3.2

3.3.2 Define the Network

If the empty template is selected, no additional network definitions need to be defined. However, if one of the other templates is selected, follow these steps to define the network properties (the properties list is different in each template):

1) Select 'Networks' from the tree view at the left.

2) Right-click on 'new1' and select Edit Network....

3) On the Attributes tab, set the attribute values for this network.

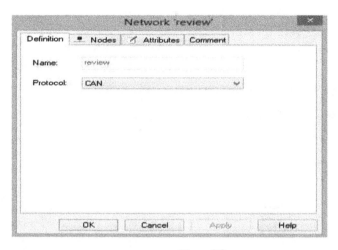

Figure 3.3

3.4 Create the Database Nodes

1) Select "Network Nodes" from the tree view on the left. Right click on it and select New. Name the first node "EMS" , "ENGINE" , "LIGHT" , "NAVIGATORS" and "SPEEDOMETER". Then, click [OK].

2) Save the database via File → Save.

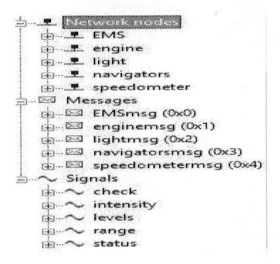

Figure 3.4

3.5 Creating Database Messages

1) Select "Messages" in the tree view on the left, right-click on it, and select New.

2) Name the first message "emsmsg" , "enginemsg" , "lightmsg" , "navigatorsmsg" and "speedometermsg".

3) Select CAN Standard (11 bit) in the *Type:* drop down menu

4) Set the DLC (Data Length Code) to 1.

5) Select the Transmitters tab and click [Add] to add a transmitter to send our message. Select the network node and add respective nodes and then click [OK].

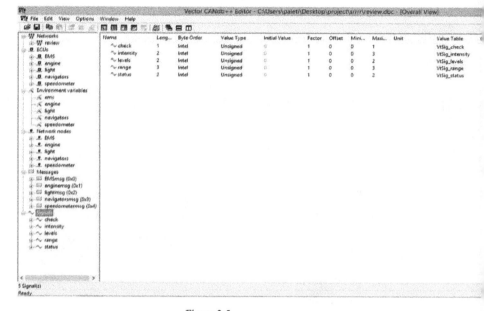

Figure 3.5

3.6 Creating Database Message Content

3.6.1 Create an EMS message

Signals are variables that occupy the data field space of a message. Our level signal will indicate whether oil level is empty, medium and full in our first message. To do this, proceed as follows:

1) In the CANdb++ Editor, select "Signals" in the tree view on the left. Right-click on it and select New.

2) For the signal *Name*, enter "levels".

3) Enter "2" for *Length (bit)* of the message. .

4) For *Byte Order*, select "Intel" .

5) Select "unsigned" for the *Value Type*.

22

6) Make sure to set "Minimum" to 0 and "Maximum" to 2.

7) Now, switch to the Messages tab and click the [Add] button. Select our message (the only one there) and click [OK]. Click [OK] to exit the dialog.

Next, we want 00 , 01 and 02 to represent the levels being either "empty" or "medium" or "full" . To do this,

1) Select View → Value Tables.

2) Right-click anywhere on the empty page and select New.

3) Name the value table, "ems".

4) Switch to the Value Descriptions tab and click the [Add] button.

5) For the value "0x0" which appears, click on "Description for the value '0x0'". Replace it with the word "empty".

6) Click the [Add] button again. This time replace "Description for the value '0x1'" with the word "medium".

7) Click the [Add] button again. This time replace "Description for the value '0x2'" with the word "full".

8) Click [OK] to exit the dialog. The value table "ems" now appears in the window.

9) Go back to the Overall View window.

3.6.2 Create an ENGINE message

Signals are variables that occupy the data field space of a message. Our check signal will indicate whether engine is not working and working properly in our first message. To do this, proceed as follows:

1) In the CANdb++ Editor, select "Signals" in the tree view on the left. Right-click on it and select New.

2) For the signal *Name*, enter "check".

3) Enter "1" for *Length (bit)* of the message. .

4) For *Byte Order*, select "Intel" .

23

5) Select "unsigned" for the *Value Type*.

6) Make sure to set "Minimum" to 0 and "Maximum" to 1.

7) Now, switch to the Messages tab and click the [Add] button. Select our message (the only one there) and click [OK]. Click [OK] to exit the dialog.

Next, we want 00 and 01 to represent the levels being either "working" or "not working" . To do this,

1) Select View → Value Tables.

2) Right-click anywhere on the empty page and select New.

3) Name the value table, "enginee".

4) Switch to the Value Descriptions tab and click the [Add] button.

5) For the value "0x0" which appears, click on "Description for the value '0x0'". Replace it with the word "not working".

6) Click the [Add] button again. This time replace "Description for the value '0x1'" with the word "working".

7) Click [OK] to exit the dialog. The value table "ems" now appears in the window.

8) Go back to the Overall View window.

3.6.3 Create LIGHT message

Signals are variables that occupy the data field space of a message. Our intensity signal will indicate whether intensity is off ,dim , bright and infinity in our first message. To do this, proceed as follows:

1) In the CANdb++ Editor, select "Signals" in the tree view on the left. Right-click on it and select New.

2) For the signal *Name*, enter "intensity".

3) Enter "2" for *Length (bit)* of the message. .

4) For *Byte Order*, select "Intel" .

5) Select "unsigned" for the *Value Type*.

6) Make sure to set "Minimum" to 0 and "Maximum" to 2.

7) Now, switch to the Messages tab and click the [Add] button. Select our message (the only one there) and click [OK]. Click [OK] to exit the dialog.

Next, we want 00 , 01, 02 and 03 to represent the levels being either "empty" or "medium" or "full" . To do this,

1) Select View → Value Tables.

2) Right-click anywhere on the empty page and select New.

3) Name the value table, "lighht".

4) Switch to the Value Descriptions tab and click the [Add] button.

5) For the value "0x0" which appears, click on "Description for the value '0x0'". Replace it with the word "off".

6) Click the [Add] button again. This time replace "Description for the value '0x1'" with the word "dim".

7) Click the [Add] button again. This time replace "Description for the value '0x2'" with the word "bright".

8) Click the [Add] button again. This time replace "Description for the value '0x3'" with the word "infinity".

9)Click [OK] to exit dialog. The value table "lighht" appears in the window.

10) Go back to the Overall View window.

3.6.4 Create NAVIGATOR message

Signals are variables that occupy the data field space of a message. Our status signal will indicate whether status is left , right and standby in our first message. To do this, proceed as follows:

1) In the CANdb++ Editor, select "Signals" in the tree view on the left. Right-click on it and select New.

2) For the signal *Name*, enter "status".

3) Enter "2" for *Length (bit)* of the message. .

4) For *Byte Order*, select "Intel" .

5) Select "unsigned" for the *Value Type*.

6) Make sure to set "Minimum" to 0 and "Maximum" to 2.

7) Now, switch to the Messages tab and click the [Add] button. Select our message (the only one there) and click [OK]. Click [OK] to exit the dialog.

Next, we want 00 , 01 and 02 to represent the levels being either "left" or "right" or "standby" . To do this,

1) Select View → Value Tables.

2) Right-click anywhere on the empty page and select New.

3) Name the value table, "navi".

4) Switch to the Value Descriptions tab and click the [Add] button.

5) For the value "0x0" which appears, click on "Description for the value '0x0'". Replace it with the word "left".

6) Click the [Add] button again. This time replace "Description for the value '0x1'" with the word "right".

7) Click the [Add] button again. This time replace "Description for the value '0x2'" with the word "standby".

8) Click [OK] to exit the dialog. The value table "ems" now appears in the window.

9) Go back to the Overall View window.

3.6.5 Create SPEEDOMETER message

Signals are variables that occupy the data field space of a message. Our range signal will indicate whether range is from , right and standby in our first message. To do this, proceed as follows:

1) In the CANdb++ Editor, select "Signals" in the tree view on the left. Right-click on it and select New.

2) For the signal *Name*, enter "status".

3) Enter "7" for *Length (bit)* of the message. .

4) For *Byte Order*, select "Intel" .

5) Select "unsigned" for the *Value Type*.

6) Make sure to set "Minimum" to 0 and "Maximum" to 127.

7) Now, switch to the Messages tab and click the [Add] button. Select our message (the only one there) and click [OK]. Click [OK] to exit the dialog.

Next, we want 00 to 09 to represent the levels from 0-100 in steps of 10. To do this,

1) Select View → Value Tables.

2) Right-click anywhere on the empty page and select New.

3) Name the value table, "range".

4) Switch to the Value Descriptions tab and click the [Add] button.

5) For the value "0x0" which appears, click on "Description for the value '0x0'. Replace it with the word "10".

6) Click the [Add] button again. This time replace "Description for the value '0x1' with the word "20".

7) Click the [Add] button again. This time replace "Description for the value '0x2' with the word "30".

8) Click the [Add] button again. This time replace "Description for the value '0x3' with the word "40".

9) Click the [Add] button again. This time replace "Description for the value '0x4' with the word "50".

10) Click the [Add] button again. This time replace "Description for the value '0x5' with the word "60".

11) Click the [Add] button again. This time replace "Description for the value '0x6' with the word "70".

12) Click the [Add] button again. This time replace "Description for the value '0x7' with the word "80".

13) Click the [Add] button again. This time replace "Description for the value '0x8' with the word "90".

14) Click the [Add] button again. This time replace "Description for the value '0x9'" with the word "100".

15) Click [OK] to exit the dialog. The value table "range" now appears in the window.

16) Go back to the Overall View window.

3.6.6 Create Database Environment Variables for Nodes

1) Select "Environment variables" in the tree view at the left, right-click on it, and select **New**.

2) Name the environment variables "ems","engine","light","navigators" and "speedometer".

3) Expand the Access drop-down list and select Read/Write

4) Expand the Value Table drop-down list and select respective value tables.

5) Change Maximum value to "0x2" , "0x1" , " 0x2" , "0x3" and "0x10" respectively.

6) Go to the Control units tab and click [Add].

7) Select control unit "EMS", "ENGINE" , "LIGHT" , "NAVIGATORS" and "SPEEDOMETER" and click [OK].

8) Click [Apply] and then click [OK] to finish.

28

3.7 Associate the Database

1) Go to CANoe and select the menu command **Window** → **Simulation Setup** to make sure the Simulation Setup window can be seen, if necessary.

2) Expand the tree list to the right and select *Databases*. Right-click on it and select **Add**.

3) Associate the "new1.dbc" database file.

3.8 Add Nodes to the Network

1) In the left half of the window, click on the connection lines to the left of the PC Board called "Bus CAN". Right-click on it and select **Insert network node**. A new node will appear on the network with the default name "ECU 1".

2) Right-click on this new node and select **Configuration…**.

3) Expand the *CANdb Name* drop down list and select the node names EMS, light, engine, navigators and speedometer Click **[Ok]**. The node name should change from "ECU 1" to "EMS". The new node will appear in the tree list to the right.

Add the other nodes in the same manner.

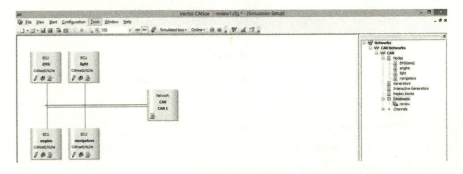

Figure 3.6

3.9 Create Panels

Designing nodes that use graphic control panels is a major feature of CANoe. These panels can be a data source or sink for system-level or node-level I/O. The values of discrete and continuous environment variables can be changed interactively on these panels during the simulation. Signal values can also be changed since Version 5.0 of CANoe.

Overlapping control and display elements can all be placed anywhere on the panel. Each panel control element must have an environment variable or signal from the database assigned to it. We will focus only on environment variables in this tutorial.

Panels are saved in CANoe panel file format (default extension .xvp or .cnp) and can then be loaded in the simulation system.

Figure 3.7

3.9.1 Panel Designer

1) To open the Panel Designer, click on the icon with a blue meter on the main toolbar of CANoe, or simply go to the File menu

2) On the menu bar of Panel Designer, select **File → Save Panel As**.

3) Using the extension .xvp and the path to the new directory, name the file "aaa.xvp". Click **[Save]**. "aaa" will be the title of the Panel when displayed in CANoe.

30

3.9.2 Adding the tools

To add a panel switch, push button and indicator switch, the steps are exactly the same for each switch. The following steps show how to add a panel switch.

1) On the top-right side, there should be a *Toolbox* section. Scroll down the list of Vector Standard Controls and double click on "Switch". A box with a dashed border should appear in the middle grey box.

2) On the bottom right side, the properties of this switch should be displayed in the Properties section and required changes in properties section.

3) To select an image to use for this switch, scroll down the Properties section. Under the Settings section, click on (highlight) Image. Next, click on the button to the right of "Choose Image…" and select the image to use.

3.9.3 Panel Editor

1) To open the Panel Editor, select File→Open Panel Editor.

2) On the menu bar of the Panel Editor, go to Options → Window setting.., which opens the *Window size, name, colors, and fonts* dialog. All we will do here for now is to give the panel a name. For the panel name, use "aaaPanel". Click [OK].

3) On the menu bar, select File → Save As. Using the extension .cnp and the path to the "new1" directory, name the file "aaa.cnp". Click [OK].

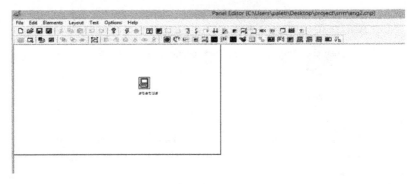

Figure 3.8

31

3.10 Place the Panels into the CANoe Environment

Next, we move back into the CANoe application to get our new panels interconnected.

1) In CANoe, select the menu command **Configuration → Panel Configuration**.

2) Click the **[Add...]** button.

3) Locate the panel files aaa.cnp and bbb.cnp in the new directory. Using the <Shift> key, click both panels and open them.

4) Expand the drop down list next to *Window type for newly configured panels* and select "Standard Window". This will create a new window outside of CANoe for each panel. ("MDI Window" will display the panels inside the CANoe program environment.)

5) Click **[OK]**.

Figure 3.9

3.11 Create Node Behavior

Next, we use the CAPL programming language feature of CANoe to give behavior to our two nodes.

A CAPL program is usually developed in the CAPL Browser. The Browser window is subdivided into three distinctive areas, or panes. The left pane contains a tree view of all important elements for which a CAPL program can be written. The area on the upper right is where global variables will be placed for the CAPL program, and the area below it is where the actual source code for each event procedure is written

3.11.1 CAPL code for EMS node

```
variables
{
  message EMSmsg emsg;
}
on key 'd'
{
  write("empty");
  output(emsg);
}
on key 'e'
{
  write("medium");
   output(emsg);

}
on key 'f'
{
  write("full");
   output(emsg);
}
```

3.11.2 CAPL code for ENGINE node

```
variables
{
  message enginemsg emsg;
}

on key F4
```

```
{
write (" engine is on");
output(emsg);
}
```

3.11.3 CAPL code for LIGHT node

```
variables
{
  message lightmsg lmsg;
}
on key 'a'
{
  write ("light is dim");
  output(lmsg);
}
on key 'b'
{
   write ("light is bright");
  output(lmsg);
}
on key 'c'
{
   write ("light is infinity");
  output(lmsg);
}
```

3.11.4 CAPL code for NAVIGATORS node

```
variables
{
  message navigatorsmsg nmsg;
}
on key F1
{
  write("left navigator");
  output(nmsg);
}
on key F2
{
```

```
  write("stand by");
   output(nmsg);


}
on key F3
{
  write("right navigator");
   output(nmsg);
}
```

3.11.5 CAPL code for SPEEDOMETER node

```
variables
{
  message speedometermsg smsg;
}

on key 'a'
{
  write ("10");
  output(smsg);
}
on key 'b'
{
   write ("20");
  output(smsg);
}
on key 'c'
{
   write ("30");
  output(smsg);
}
on key 'd'
{
  write ("40");
  output(smsg);
}
on key 'e'
{
```

```
    write ("50");
  output(smsg);
}
on key 'f'
{
    write ("60");
  output(smsg);
}
on key 'g'
{
  write ("70");
  output(smsg);
}
on key 'h'
{
    write ("80");
  output(smsg);
}
on key 'i'
{
    write ("90");
  output(smsg);
}
on key 'j'
{
  write ("100");
  output(smsg);
}
```

CHAPTER 4

HARDWARE SETUP AND PROCESS STEPS

4.1 TZM-toolset-MPC5567(Eclipse IDE NEXUS)

To make ECU functioned it needs to be programmed. The C language is suitable for embedded system design project because the users can see the structure of the moduled operations. The programming includes initializing the MPC5567, configuring the LEDs, initializing the CAN port. There are a lot of C compilers available but Eclipse IDE was chosen because it had been developed with the same manufacturer with the microchip MPC5567.

Eclipse Integrated Development Environment (IDE) is a free, integrated MPC based toolset for the development of embedded applications. The eclipse IDE runs as 64-bit application on Microsoft Windows and includes several free software components for application development, hardware, emulation and debugging. Eclipse IDE supports both Assembly and C programming languages. C language is often used with microcontrollers because of small size high speed and the access it allows to the real world.

Figure 4.1

4.1.1 Burning the program into MPC5567:

We must have a programmer (hardware) to connect the PC to MPC5567 for programming there are several programmers available in the market but the best programmers are those with USB. PPCNEXUS supports all official programmers from the manufacturer of the MPC's.

Steps for burning the code into MPC5567

- Connect USB to the PC and the other end of the USB should be connected to the JTAG port of the Flexdevel board and ensure that both the lights in the indicator glow.
- Open NEXUS in the window refresh and connect to the Flexdevel kit.
- Once MPC5567 is connected go to configure and automated script options, run the script file after the debugger resets the Flexdevel
- In the high level load, Click on process load command and select .elf file of built program.
- Now click on Source go and wait till the code is burnt.

38

4.1.2 Flowchart for the program

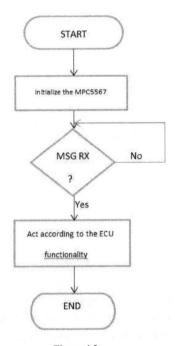

Figure 4.2

4.1.3 Flowchart explanation:

For each of the ECU's programs start with initializing the MPC5567 and CAN. The MPC5567 now checks for successful reception of the transmitted message. The message is received it acts accordingly with the ECUs functionality (for ex: LIGHT ECU if 00, 01, 02 is transmitted then they must reflect the LED). If message is not received then it must wait until it receives the message.

4.2 Flow chart for monitoring the hardware with CANoe (software):

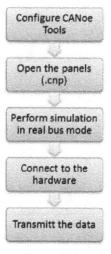

Figure 4.3

CANoe is a Windows based application provided by Vector. This software is designed to interact with hardware . In this project the hardware ECUs are triggered by this software. As detailed in Chapter 3 configure the CANoe tools. Now open the created panels(.cnp). It must be noted while doing the hardware the mode of operation has to be in real bus mode. Connect to the hardware and simulate in the software. Now transmit the required message and check the result.

CHAPTER 5

RESULTS AND ANALYSIS

Based on the results, the objective for developing simulation and test system for vehicle body CAN bus using CANoe has been achieved. The project demonstrated that implementing CAN network using both CANoe (software) and FlexDevel kits (hardware) can be done successfully. As stated in Chapter 3, five nodes are created i.e. EMS, Engine, Light, Navigators and Speedometer. Both the hardware and software outputs are shown below for each of the node (ECU).

5.1 EMS (Engine Monitoring System):

In real time there are many things that can be monitored for an engine of which the main is oil level. In the project there are three levels for the oil namely low, medium and high represented by led 03, 04, 02 of the led panel on board .On varying the dip switches one can change the message , the message is transmitted via a CANcase XL to the Vector CANoe and results can be seen in trace window.

Hardware Output:

5.1 EMS low

5.2 EMS medium

5.3 EMS full

Software output:

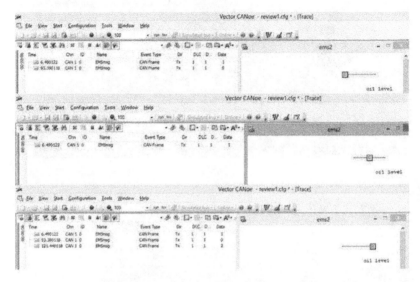

5.4 EMS software output

5.2 Engine

In the project there are two levels for the Engine namely on and off. They are represented by 02 and 03 LED's of LED panel on board. On varying the dip switches one can change the message, the message is transmitted via a CANcase XL to the Vector CANoe and results can be seen in trace window.

5.5 Engine off

5.6 Engine on

Software Output:

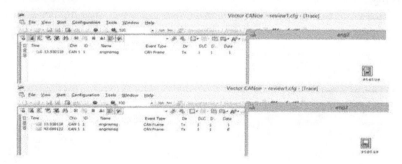

5.7 Engine software output

5.8 Trace window in CANoe for EMS and Engine ECU's

5.3 Light

In the project there are four levels for the oil namely off, dim, bright and infinity represented by led 03,02,05 and 04 of the led panel on board .On varying the dip switches one can change the message , the message is transmitted via a CANcase XL to the Vector CANoe and results can be seen in trace window.

5.9 Light off

5.10 Light bright

5.11 Light Infinity

Software output:

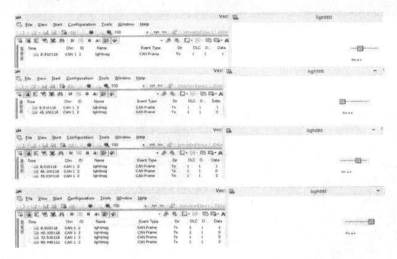

5.12 Light ECU in software

5.4 Navigators

In the project there are three levels for the navigators namely left, stand by and right represented by led 04,03,02 of the led panel on board .On varying the dip switches one can change the message , the message is transmitted via a CANcase XL to the Vector CANoe and results can be seen in trace window.

5.13 Navigators-left

5.14 Navigators-Standby

5.15 Navigators-Right

Software output:

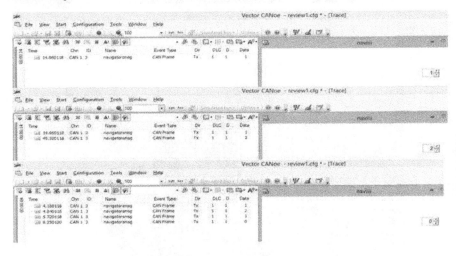

5.16 Navigator in software

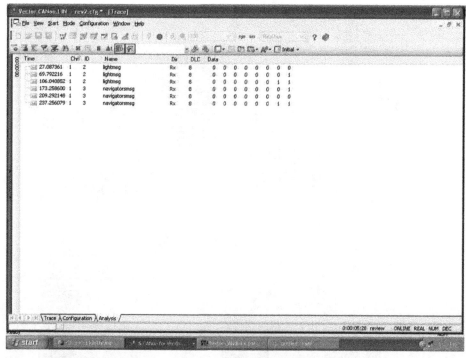

5.17 Trace window in CANoe for Light and Navigator ECU's

5.5 Speedometer

In the project there are nine levels for the speedometer namely 10,20,30,40,50,60,70,80 and 90 represented by led 01,02,03,04,05,06,02 and 03,03 and 04,04 and 05 of the led panel on board .On varying the dip switches one can change the message , the message is transmitted via a CANcase XL to the Vector CANoe and results can be seen in trace window.

5.18 Speedometer-10

5.19 Speedometer-20

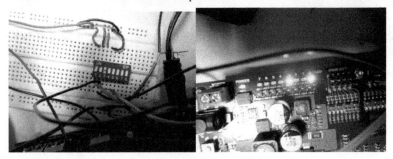

5.20 Speedometer-30

5.21 Speedometer-40

5.22 Speedometer-50

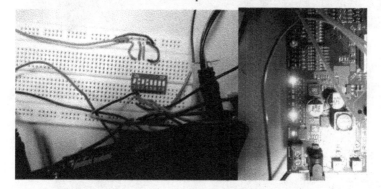

5.23 Speedometer-60

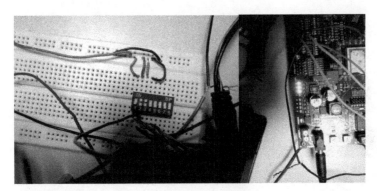

5.24 Speedometer-70

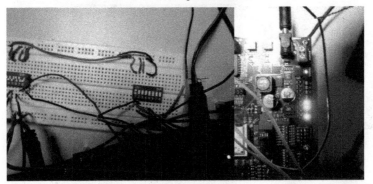

5.25 Speedometer-80

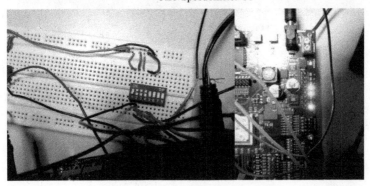

5.26 Speedometer-90

Software output:

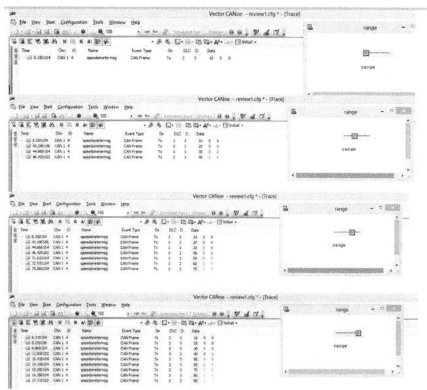

5.27 Speedometer in software

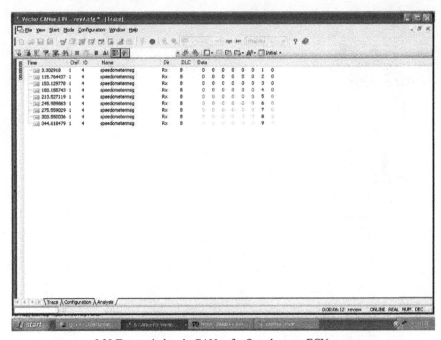

5.28 Trace window in CANoe for Speedometer ECU

CHAPTER 6

Conclusion and Future Work

6.1 Conclusion

The project "SIMULATION AND TEST SYSTEM FOR VEHICLE BODY CAN-BUS"
had been successfully designed and tested. It has been developed by integrated features of
all the hardware components used. Presence of every module had been reasoned out and
placed carefully thus contributing to the best working of the unit.

Firstly, we have created a software version of all the ECU's in the software
platform CANoe 7.6 and successfully simulated them and obtained the results. Secondly,
using FlexDevel MPC5567 boards we have implemented CAN network created in the
software platform where each of the board is programmed with a functional ECU. The
hardware is tested with help of an interface CANCase XL that helps it to connect to the
software Vector CANoe 7.6 .

Finally the results from software and hardware are compared and analyzed .Thus
making CANoe a favorable environment for *SIMULATION AND TEST SYSTEM FOR
VEHICLE BODY CAN-BUS.*

6.2 Future work

As a part of further developments we can use more number of sensors in the hardware
platform i.e. gas sensors, oil level detectors etc. Further, real time simulation can be
supported by integrating with the help of an OBD(On Board Diagnostics)simulator.
Within the software further concepts of wireless CAN.

REFERENCES:

[1]   Hanxing Chen and Jun Tian, "Research on the Controller Area Network", International conference on Networking and Digital Society, pp. 251-254, 2009.

[2]   Fang Zhou, Shuqin Li, Xia Hou "Development Method of Simulation and Test System for Vehicle Body CAN Bus Based on CANoe" *(IEEE paper* Proceedings of the 7th World Congress on Intelligent Control and Automation June 25 - 27, 2008, Chongqing, China).

[3] Wu Kuanming. The Theory and Design of Application System of CAN Bus. Beijing: Beijing University of Aeronautics and Astronautics Press, 2001. 18-34.

[4] Yang Li, Yan Weisheng, Gao Jian, Zhang Lichuan. CAN System Development Based on CANoe Measurement and Control Technology, 2007, 26(4):66-67, 75

[5] Vector Informatik GmbH. CANoe manual(version 7.6),2010.

[6] Flexdevel Board manual

[7] BOSCH CAN specification version 2.0,1991.

Referece from web:

[1] www.vector.com

[2]www.eberspacher.com

[3]www.can-cia.com

[4]www.digi.com

BIODATA:

Name	:	PALETI SRINATH
Father's Name	:	PALETI VEERA VENKATA RAO
Date of Birth	:	9th October 1990
Gender	:	Male
Address	:	H.No: 6-1-108, Flat no:206, Gharonda veera apts., PadmaraoNagar,Secunderabad Andhra Pradesh. Pin code: 500025
Phone	:	9092516835
Email	:	srinath.paleti@hotmail.com
Area of Interest	:	Embedded System Design

BIODATA:

Name	:	KANDURI SRINIVAS
Father's Name	:	KANDURI JANARDHAN
Date of Birth	:	23rd October 1992
Gender	:	Male
Address	:	H.No: 8-85-11-3, Opp.Seshaiah Qut Near Sree Rama Talkies, Dhone, Kurnool (dt) Andhra Pradesh. Pin code: 518222
Phone	:	8144881729
Email	:	kanduri_srinivas@outlook.com
Area of Interest	:	Embedded System Design